WHO REALLY DISCOVERED ELECTRICITY?

by Amie Jane Leavitt

Consultant:
Amy Fisher
PhD Candidate
History of Science and Technology
University of Minnesota
Minneapolis, Minnesota

Fact Finders are published by Capstone Press,
151 Good Counsel Drive, P.O. Box 669, Mankato, Minnesota 56002.
www.capstonepub.com

Books published by Capstone Press are manufactured with paper
containing at least 10 percent post-consumer waste.

Library of Congress Cataloging-in-Publication Data
Leavitt, Amie Jane.
 Who really discovered electricity? / by Amie Jane Leavitt.
 p. cm.—(Fact finders. Race for history)
 Summary: "Follows the stories of Dr. William Gilbert, Stephen Gray, and
Benjamin Franklin as they explore the force now called electricity"—Provided by publisher.
 Includes bibliographical references and index.
 ISBN 978-1-4296-3345-1 (lib. bdg.)
 ISBN 978-1-4296-6248-2 (paperback)
 1. Electricity—History—Juvenile literature. 2. Gilbert, William, 1544-1603—Juvenile literature. 3. Gray,
Stephen, 1666-1736—Juvenile literature. 4. Franklin, Benjamin, 1706-1790—Juvenile literature. I. Title. II.
Series.
 QC527.2.L43 2011
 537.09—dc22   2010026029

Editorial Credits
Jennifer Besel, editor; Alison Thiele, series designer; Bobbie Nuytten, book designer;
    Wanda Winch, media researcher; Eric Manske, production specialist

Photo Credits
Alamy: Mary Evans Picture Library, 15, North Wind Picture Archives, 21, World History
Archive, 18; The Bridgeman Art Library International: ©Look and Learn/Private Collection/Peter
Jackson, 25, Private Collection/Arthur Ackland Hunt, 17, 26; Getty Images: SSPL, 23; John D. Jenkins,
www.sparkmuseum.com, 13; Library of Congress: Prints and Photographs Division, cover (top left,
bottom), 5 (top, middle); Mary Evans Picture Library, 6; Nova Development Corp., 28-29 (all); ©The
Royal Society, cover (top right), 5 (bottom), 24; Shutterstock: Sergey Furtaev, cover (bulb), U.P. images
(banner), Wikipedia, 8, 11

Printed in the United States of America in Stevens Point, Wisconsin.
092010   005934WZS11

TABLE OF CONTENTS

THE RACE

Lightbulbs glow. Computers hum. Electricity energizes almost everything in our modern world. But people didn't always have use of this power. In fact, it was a long time before people even understood what electricity was.

In ancient times, the Greeks knew that a substance called **amber** had special qualities. If rubbed with cloth or fur, amber attracts straw and feathers. The Greeks believed amber had a soul that made it act that way.

Today we know that rubbing amber gives it a static electric **charge**. But it took a long time to figure out that fact. So who really discovered electricity? The race to understanding this power is long and full of experiments. The players are divided by decades. But only one can be the winner. Who will it be?

amber: pine sap that has hardened into a yellowish-brown material

charge: an amount of electricity

MEET THE PLAYERS

BENJAMIN FRANKLIN

A writer, printer, and scientist—he lives in Philadelphia, in the American colonies, in the mid-1700s. He has retired from his printing business and now spends time studying science.

DR. WILLIAM GILBERT

A doctor—he lives in England in the late 1500s and early 1600s. During the day, he treats patients. But at night, he conducts experiments in his home laboratory.

STEPHEN GRAY

A retired fabric dyer—he has an interest in natural science. He's studied astronomy and has made several discoveries about sunspots. He lives in England in the late 1600s and early 1700s.

CHAPTER ONE

A SPECIAL POWER

Gilbert in his laboratory

Gilbert's Magnetic Idea

William Gilbert is a doctor unlike any other of his time. Now in 1583, most people believe that anything unusual is magical. But Gilbert is different. He experiments to find answers about the world. One of Gilbert's interests is the **magnetic** rock lodestone. Gilbert doesn't believe lodestones get power from magic. He doesn't know what causes their power. But he's spent the last several years trying to find out.

In his experiments, Gilbert has learned a lot about magnets. He's proven that magnets attract only iron objects. According to his experiments, magnets work in all kinds of weather. And the Earth itself is like a giant magnet.

Gilbert wants to further his experiments with magnets. He studies what the ancient Greeks knew about amber. The Greeks found that if they rubbed amber with fur, it would pull lightweight materials toward it. Gilbert wonders if amber and lodestone have the same power. He suspects they don't because lodestone doesn't need to be rubbed. But he has to find out for sure.

RACE FACT Many historians consider Gilbert the first scientist of the modern world. He was the first to use experiments to prove his ideas.

magnetic: attracted to iron or steel

Gray's Goal

It's 1729 in England. Stephen Gray has heard about a power that sparks from objects. But very little has been learned about it. Gray has also seen a **friction** machine that demonstrates the power. The machine has a glass sphere that is turned by a crank. When a piece of leather is held against the spinning sphere, golden sparks leap from the glass. Feathers and foil are pulled toward it.

Most people think this power is nothing more than entertainment. But Gray thinks there could be more to it. He wants to study the power to find out what it can really do.

demonstration of a friction machine

friction: the force produced when two objects rub against each other

Franklin's Spark

It's a summer evening in 1743. Benjamin Franklin watches in amazement as a showman performs his final trick. Silk cords dangle from the ceiling. The man ties the cords around a boy's ankles and wrists, suspending him in midair. Then he rubs the boy's bare feet with a glass tube. Suddenly, the showman touches the boy's forehead. Golden sparks flicker out. The audience applauds. It must be magic!

Franklin has heard of this power, but has never seen it in action. The power is a mystery to most scientists. Many don't think it's anything more than a circus act. But this power seems like more than a parlor trick to Franklin.

Franklin gathers scientific instruments and begins to study the sparking power. His friend gives him a friction machine that makes sparks just like in the trick. One day Franklin notices that the sparks coming from the machine's glass look similar to lightning bolts. Could lightning hold the key to this strange power?

RACE FACT

Franklin had a fun sense of humor. He created a metal spider that would hop around when charged with electricity.

CHAPTER TWO

TESTING IDEAS

Gilbert's Amber Experiment

Back in England, Gilbert struggles with a question of his own. Could the differences between amber and lodestone mean they have different powers? In order to find out, Gilbert invents a device to detect amber's power. His **versorium** has a rotating metal needle balanced on a sharp point. When Gilbert moves a rubbed piece of amber toward the machine, the needle rotates toward the amber.

Gilbert makes versoriums out of many kinds of metal. All the metals spin toward the rubbed amber. These results are very different from the magnetic lodestone. Lodestones only attract iron. Gilbert now knows the powers of amber and lodestone definitely have different qualities.

versorium: a tool that rotates toward objects with electrical charges

Gilbert goes back to his research. Has anyone else studied this? He can't find any name for amber's unique power. The Greek word for amber is *elektron*. So Gilbert decides to call amber and any other object with this power an electric. He calls the power itself electrical movement.

Now he has a name for the power. But he's still not sure if electrical movement is a type of magnetism. And are there other objects that act like amber? How can he find out?

Gilbert's versorium

Gray's Long Experiment

This strange power has Gray asking questions too. He begins to research and finds the works of William Gilbert. He learns that Gilbert called objects with this power electrics. But Gilbert didn't study what electrics can do. Gray intends to find out.

He finds a glass tube in his scientific supplies. Then he sticks a cork into each end to keep out dust. After rubbing the glass with silk, he dangles it over a feather. The feather instantly floats toward the tube. Gray isn't surprised by this. The friction machine showed that a feather would stick to glass. What amazes him is that the feather also sticks to the corks. He has just discovered that the electrical power can move from the glass tube to the corks!

Gray forms a **theory**. He thinks if an electric touches another object, that object will become an electric too. But how far can the power go?

Gray sets to work answering his question. First, he attaches an ivory ball to the end of a stick. He pushes the stick into one of the corks in the glass tube. Then he rubs the tube and hovers the ball over a feather. The feather rises up to the ball and the stick! He adds longer sticks. Each time the ball picks up the feather.

theory: an idea that explains something that is unknown
hemp: a plant whose fibers are used to make rope

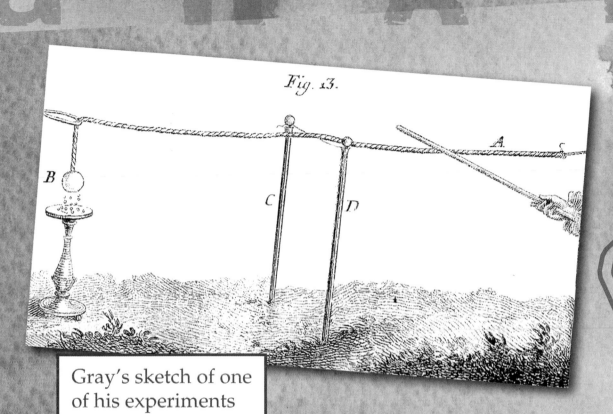

Fig. 13.

B

C

D

A

Gray's sketch of one of his experiments

When the sticks are too long, they begin to sag. Gray decides to use a long **hemp** string between the tube and ivory ball. He hangs the string and ball vertically over the railing of a 34-foot (10-meter) high balcony. Just as before, he rubs the glass. A pile of brass foil floats toward the ball.

Gray knows he's onto something big. But he can't test any further. The balcony is the tallest point on the house. He wonders if the power will work if he runs the string horizontally. There's only one way to find out.

Franklin's Stormy Experiment

Just like Gray, Franklin researches and experiments with the power. He studies the works of William Gilbert and Stephen Gray. He learns from their experiments that metal attracts the power. He also learns that some materials, like silk, won't carry it. Franklin also discovers that Gilbert called this power electrical movement. Now he understands why some people call this strange power electricity.

Franklin decides to make a kite to send up to the clouds during a storm. On top of the kite, he attaches a metal wire. The metal will attract this electricity—if that's what lightning is. From the center of the kite, he ties a long string. An iron key dangles from the bottom. Finally, he ties a silk ribbon to the end of the string. If the power does run down the string, it won't pass through the silk.

On a stormy June day in 1752, Franklin and his son, William, journey into a field. Dark clouds billow overhead. William releases the kite into the air. Holding the silk, he runs back to his father who is standing in an old shed.

The kite jerks in the strong wind. Suddenly, Franklin notices something. The string's fibers are standing on end! Instantly, Franklin remembers something that happened in his laboratory. One time, his thin, brown hair stood on end when he was near his charged glass globe. Could this mean what he thinks it does?

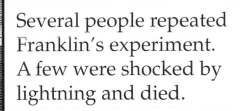

Several people repeated Franklin's experiment. A few were shocked by lightning and died.

CHAPTER THREE

GETTING SOME ANSWERS

Gilbert's Startling Observations

An idea for an experiment hits Gilbert like a bolt of lightning. He decides to see if other objects have the same power as amber. He experiments with a variety of objects. Diamonds, glass, and wax move the versorium when rubbed with fur too. He also discovers that these objects pick up lightweight materials such as fibers and feathers. Lodestones can't do that. They only pick up iron objects.

He also discovers that the power in amber doesn't work in certain kinds of weather. If it's a warm, rainy day, the amber hardly moves the versorium. Weather has no effect on lodestone.

Gilbert now knows for sure this electric movement isn't magnetic. He's made a huge discovery!

Gilbert demonstrating his discoveries

Franklin Gets Zapped

Franklin is still trying to get an answer to his question too. The fibers of his kite's string are standing on end. Is it possible that lightning struck the kite's metal wire, charging the string's fibers with electricity? Franklin decides the best way to find out is to see for himself. If lightning is electricity, sparks will fly from the key when he touches it. Franklin inches his knuckle forward.

Zap! Before Franklin's skin touches the iron key, a spark shocks him. He rubs the feeling back into his hand and smiles at his son. They both know that Franklin was right. Lightning is electricity!

RACE FACT Franklin came up with several terms that we still use when talking about electricity today, including "battery," "charged," "plus," and "minus."

Franklin felt a zap of electricity before he even touched the key.

CHAPTER FOUR

CHANGING THE WORLD

Gilbert Tells the World

Gilbert decides to write a book to share his discoveries. He spent many, many years studying magnets. He observed things no one else has ever noticed. Now it's time to tell the world what he's learned.

He calls his book *De Magnete*. He spends most of the book explaining how his theories on magnets are true. He dedicates a small section of the book to his discovery of electrics. His book is published in 1600. But just three years later, Gilbert dies. He never knows how his discovery changes the world.

RACE FACT

In 1600, Gilbert became the personal doctor for Queen Elizabeth I. He died of the plague in 1603.

a sketch drawn by Gilbert for his book, *De Magnete*

23

Gray's elevated boy experiment

Gray's Search for a Final Distance

Gray thinks understanding electrics could change the world. He searches for a distance where the power stops moving. The farthest distance he gets it to travel is 866 feet (264 m). By 1730, he's ready to move on to answering other questions about electrical movement.

Gray experiments to see if the power can go through the human body. He discovers that it can! Gray gives demonstrations, showing how electric power travels through an elevated boy. He hangs a boy up by his wrists and ankles. Then he rubs the child's feet with a glass tube. Foil pieces are attracted to the boy's head. When he touches the boy's forehead, sparks fly out. This demonstration becomes a popular trick in scientific shows throughout the rest of the 1700s.

Franklin installing
a lightning rod

Franklin's Electric Discoveries

Franklin's discovery that lightning is electricity changes the world of science. The new information has everyone, including Franklin, wondering what else there is to learn about this power.

Franklin continues experimenting. He spends time studying how electricity works and how it can be used. He shows that electricity can move in one direction or back and forth. Franklin also designs the lightning rod. This metal pole is placed on buildings to protect them from lightning strikes. He knows he has come a long way from his first introduction to electricity—a spark from the forehead of a boy.

THE WINNER

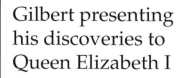

Gilbert presenting his discoveries to Queen Elizabeth I

All three players in our race made discoveries in the field of electricity. But only one can be the winner. Who really discovered electricity? The winner is William Gilbert.

Gilbert determined that the forces from lodestones and amber were distinctly different. He also invented the first equipment to test electricity. And he gave the power the name we still use today.

Gray also contributed to the field of electricity. He found that electricity can move from one object to another. He also learned some materials absorb electrical power and some don't. Gray knew about Gilbert's work and drew on it to make his own discoveries.

Franklin used the works of Gilbert and Gray in his experiments with electricity. Many people think Franklin discovered electricity with his kite experiment. Although that's not true, he did introduce the world to many new ideas about electricity. People still use lightning rods to protect their homes. And his discoveries of how electricity moves make our modern uses of electricity possible.

Scientists continue to study electricity today. They are looking for new ways to make it and cleaner ways to use it. In fact, you could say the race to discover more about electricity is still being run.

TIMELINE

600 BC — The ancient Greeks begin writing about amber and its unusual power.

1663 — Otto von Guericke invents a friction machine that uses a sulfur ball turned by a crank. When rubbed, the ball attracts lightweight objects, showing the power of electrics.

600 BC

1600 — William Gilbert publishes his book *De Magnete*, in which he describes the objects he names electrics.

AD 1583 — William Gilbert begins experimenting with magnets and amber.

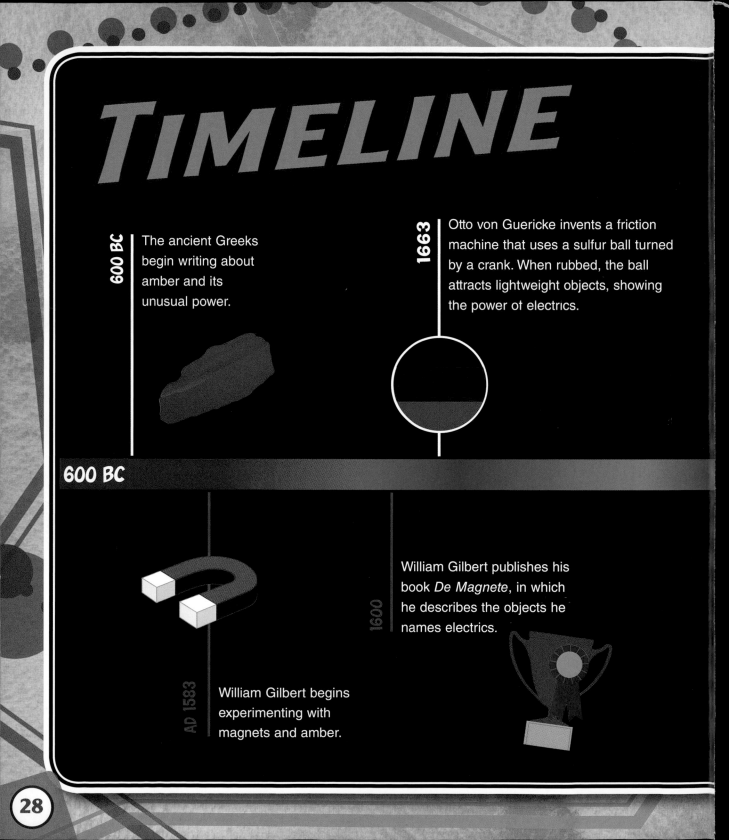

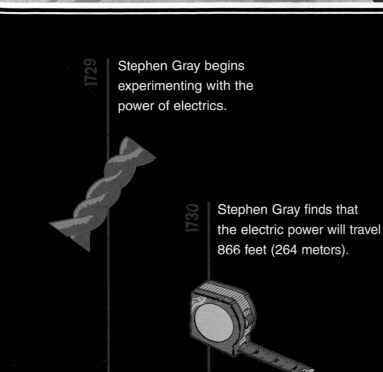

1729 Stephen Gray begins experimenting with the power of electrics.

1752 Benjamin Franklin conducts his kite experiment. He also invents the lightning rod.

1730 Stephen Gray finds that the electric power will travel 866 feet (264 meters).

AD 1752

1706 Francis Hauksbee invents a friction machine that uses a glass globe instead of a sulfur ball.

1743 Benjamin Franklin sees his first electrics show.

1747 Benjamin Franklin begins extensive experiments with electricity in his home laboratory.

GLOSSARY

amber (AM-buhr)—pine sap that has hardened over millions of years into a yellowish-brown material

charge (CHARJ)—an amount of electricity running through something

friction (FRIK-shuhn)—the force produced when two objects rub against each other

hemp (HEMP)—a plant whose fibers are used to make rope and sacks

magnetic (mag-NET-ik)—having the attractive properties of a magnet; a magnet attracts iron or steel

theory (THEE-ur-ee)—an idea that explains something that is unknown

versorium (ver-SOR-ee-uhm)—a tool that rotates toward objects with electrical charges

READ MORE

Galiano, Dean. *Electric and Magnetic Phenomena.* Science Made Simple. New York.: Rosen Central, 2011.

Norlander, Britt. *I've Discovered Electricity!* Eureka! New York: Marshall Cavendish Benchmark., 2009.

Price, Sean Stewart. *The Story Behind Electricity.* True Stories. Chicago.: Heinemann Library, 2009.

Venezia, Mike. *Benjamin Franklin: Electrified the World with New Ideas.* Getting to Know the World's Greatest Inventors & Scientists. New York: Children's Press, 2009.

INTERNET SITES

FactHound offers a safe, fun way to find Internet sites related to this book. All of the sites on FactHound have been researched by our staff.

Here's all you do:

Visit *www.facthound.com*

Type in this code: 9781429633451

Super-cool stuff! Check out projects, games and lots more at **www.capstonekids.com**

INDEX